WORKING PAPERS

TELECOMMUNICATIONS BYPASS

AND THE "BRANDON EFFECT"

WORKING PAPER NO. 199

February 1993

BUREAU OF ECONOMICS
FEDERAL TRADE COMMISSION
WASHINGTON, DC 20580

Telecommunications Bypass and the "Brandon Effect"*

Steven G. Parsons

Southwestern Bell Telephone

Michael R. Ward

Federal Trade Commission

February, 1993

Abstract: The creation of a charge for long distance companies to access the local telephone companies' switched network created the incentive to bypass the local switched network in order to avoid access charges that were substantially above cost. This paper explores the implications of a federal regulatory policy of a target total dollar switched access revenue requirement. In particular, the paper focuses on the so called "Brandon Effect" in which bypass incentives are attenuated when there is a target total dollar switched access revenue. Empirical analysis confirms the "Brandon Effect" on bypass decisions.

---

*   The views expressed here do not necessarily reflect those of either Southwestern Bell Telephone or the Federal Trade Commission. This paper is an extension of Parsons and Ward (1991). We would like to thank Paul Brandon, Tim Daniel, Peter Griffes, Alex Larson, Doug Mudd, Bob Rogers, Richard Shin and Ken Troske for comments and suggestions and Dolly Howarth for research assistance.

1.   Introduction

The divestiture of AT&T and the FCC's order on access charges accentuated a conflict between telecommunications policy and competitive forces. In particular, prior to the divestiture of AT&T, the price of long distance service gradually grew in order to offset a growing fraction of the cost of basic local telephone service assigned to long distance operations (Johnson (1982)). After 1983, the Federal Communications Commission (FCC) maintained this subsidy by requiring long distance companies to pay a per-minute-of-use fee as part of the switched access charge.[1] Since switched access charges are substantially in excess of local exchange company costs of providing switched access, competitive pressures are driving long distance companies to seek lower priced alternative means of connecting to end users; they are seeking to "bypass" the local switched network and its attendant charges.

Long distance companies purchase telephone access, usually from the Local Exchange Companies (LECs), since long distance networks generally do not reach customers' telephones. The decision to bypass essentially entails a comparison of the long distance companies' cost of bypass and the price of switched access provided by the LEC. Previous studies have focused on the lower cost of bypass for large and geographically concentrated customers (see, for example, Bellcore (1984), Britman, et al. (1989), Brock (1984), Grandstaff and Watters (1989), Jackson and Rohlfs (1985) and USTA (1984)). In contrast, this study addresses the differences in the shadow price of switched access across long distance companies. Shadow and nominal prices for switched access could differ for a long distance company because its choice of access could affect the switched access price charged.

If the total long distance switched access revenue is known to be a constant sum, then (by regulatory fiat) a shift toward bypass from switched access by one firm will raise switched access prices for all firms. If the bypassing long distance company represents a small fraction of the switched access volume, most of the switched access price increase is borne by its competitors. If it represents a large fraction, the long distance company internalizes most of the switched access price increase. A long distance company's decision to bypass will depend,

---

[1] The long distance to local subsidy was reduced in 1985, when a Subscriber Line Charge was instituted as a recurring monthly charge to local service subscribers. However, SLC revenues currently make up only about a third of all interstate network access revenues.

1

in part, on the degree to which the attendant switched access price increase is internalized. Thus, larger long distance companies have lower shadow prices for switched access.

The attenuation of the long distance companies' incentive to bypass due to the regulators' desire to capture a fixed revenue requirement from switched access has been labeled the "Brandon Effect" after the AT&T executive who introduced the idea. Brandon (1982) is the first known reference of this phenomenon. Also, Brock (1984), on page 4, implies a variant when he states "If some companies bypass the switched access facilities and the revenue requirement to be provided by access remains constant, then access prices will be raised for the remaining customers. The higher prices will then induce further bypass and further increases until either equilibrium access price is reached . . . or all customers find alternatives to switched access." In Brock's scenario, regulators seek a fixed amount of revenue from access but the long distance companies do not consider this regulatory objective when they make bypass decisions. Katz and Willig (1985) model a version of the Brandon Effect in the context of determining if proposed long distance rates entail predatory pricing. Simnett (1988) captures a version of the Brandon Effect by constructing differing switched access shadow prices to AT&T and the other long distance companies, but he does not address the bypass implications. To our knowledge, no one has tested for the existence of the Brandon Effect.

The principle contributions of this paper are a mathematically explicit model of the Brandon Effect and an empirical verification of the existence and size of the Brandon Effect. Two variants of firm specific access/bypass demand substitution equations are estimated. The estimation procedures employed are extensions of existing instrumental variable methods for simultaneous systems of equations. The results do not uniformly confirm, but do suggest that regulators seek constant total dollar subsidies from long distance companies and these firms' bypass decisions reflect a Brandon Effect.

The next section describes some of the features of access provision in the telecommunications industry in more detail. Section 3 presents a simple model of bypass with an emphasis on the Brandon Effect and its implications. In this model, the long distance companies shadow price for switched access is equal to the nominal price times one minus the share of switched access purchased by the long distance company. Section 4 describes the testable hypotheses implied by the model and the data with which the tests were conducted. The fifth section

2

presents and discusses empirical findings for the existence and significance of the Brandon Effect. This is followed by a brief conclusion.

2.   A Description of the Access Market

A long distance telephone company operates a communications network that connects local telephone exchanges, hence, it is called an Interexchange Carrier (IC). The LECs, such as the regional Bell Operating Companies and GTE, transport long distance telephone calls between customers' premises and the nearest termination point of an ICs' network. These services are collectively called carrier access and represent nearly half of all IC costs. AT&T's 1984 divestiture effectively precluded the Bell operating companies from offering long distance service.

States regulate prices for intrastate services, and the FCC regulates prices for interstate services, such as interstate switched access. Until recently, ICs and LECs operated under rate-of-return regulation.[2] To accomplish joint regulatory oversight, some LEC assets are allocated to the intrastate and interstate jurisdictions for cost recovery in a necessarily arbitrary way. The costs assigned to the interstate jurisdiction are primarily recovered through a switched access charge on each minute of long distance connection and, beginning in 1985, a Subscriber Line Charge billed as a flat rate monthly charge on each telephone line.[3]

In *Smith v. Illinois Bell Tel. Co.* (1930), the courts ruled that since AT&T's long distance service used the local exchange network, a portion of the cost of the local network should be recovered through long distance rates. The portion of the local network assigned to long distance service steadily grew to 27% in 1982[4] with little relation

---

[2] The FCC began development of the AT&T Price Cap Plan in 1987 with Policy and Rules Concerning Rates for Dominant Carriers, CC Docket No. 87-313, Notice of Proposed Rulemaking, 2 FCC Rcd 5208 (1987). Price cap regulation for AT&T took effect in July, 1989. As a result of the FCC's Second Report and Order in CC Docket 87-313 released October 4, 1990, price caps for LECs became effective January 1, 1991. However, the LECs are still strongly tied to rate-of-return regulation, because earnings above certain thresholds results in lower future LEC prices and, thus, rates-of-return.

[3] Most special access, as well as some smaller revenue services, are also assigned to the interstate jurisdiction.

[4] Originally the proportion of the local network costs assigned to long distance operations was the fraction of calls going over long distances. In the early 1950s, this was less than 3% and by 1982 it was 8%.

to underlying economic costs.[5] The FCC's 1983 Access Charge Plan formalized this cost assignment and cost recovery mechanism with an additional charge, called a Carrier Common Line Charge, on the switching function of switched access. At first, the non-AT&T ICs had "nonpremium" connections to the LECs (e.g., customers were required to dial extra digits to reach non-AT&T ICs); the additional charge for nonpremium access was set at 45% of that for premium service obtained by AT&T. The divestiture agreement required the LECs to install equipment to provide equal access to any IC asking for it. The equal access equipment is currently in place for nearly all (91%) IC customers.[6]

In devising its access charge plan, the FCC eventually recognized that if usage-sensitive access charges greatly exceeded marginal costs, ICs and high volume customers would have an incentive to make alternate connections between the customer's premises and the IC's network in order to bypass the LEC and avoid switched access charges. Thus, the FCC decided that part of the basic local exchange costs allocated to the interstate jurisdiction should be recovered through a fixed recurring monthly Subscriber Line Charge billed to the customer rather than the usage sensitive switched access charges billed to the IC.[7] Economists had argued that these costs were incurred because customers had access to the network and did not rise with usage, thus movement toward a recurring monthly charge increased efficiency by aligning prices more closely with costs.[8] A Subscriber Line Charge was gradually instituted[9] that lowered switched access charges but did not eliminate them. In 1984, the average switched access price was $.173 per conversation minute; by 1991 it was $.072 (U.S. Federal-State Joint Board (1991).

---

[5] See also, Temin and Peters (1985a, 1985b), Griffen (1982), Kasserman, Mayo and Flynn (1990), Kahn and Shew (1987) and Johnson (1982). With respect to the history of deregulation and telecommunications policy, see generally, Brock(1981), Faulhaber (1987), Temin (1987) and Larson and Mudd (1992).

[6] However, nonpremium service still accounts for 5% of OCC service and 20% of the ICs do not purchase premium service from Bell Operating Companies (Statistics of Communications Common Carriers (1991)).

[7] The Subscriber Line Charge was established in CC Dockets 78-72, and 80-286 93 FCC 2d 241 (released February 28, 1983).

[8] See Temin (1987) on the FCC's 1983 Access Charge Plan and Wenders (1987) and Wenders and Egan (1986) on efficient pricing for access. Also see Kahn and Shew (1987).

[9] The Subscriber Line Charge has leveled off at a maximum monthly rate of $3.50 per line for residential and single line business service and $6.00 per line for multi-line business service.

The threat of bypass resulted in prices for access that more closely reflect the cost of service. One response to this threat was the imposition of the Subscriber Line Charge and concurrent reductions in switched access charges. Special access prices are based on circuit capacity rather than actual use, as with switched access, and can be thought of as volume discounts for large and more demand elastic customers. Switched access rates are averaged over geography and density, with substantial differences in the LEC's cost of service. Bypass has generally occurred where the cost of providing alternate access is the lowest. LECs have asked regulators for the ability to set prices closer to actual costs in response to bypass competition. Originally, the competition was relegated to the provision of dedicated carrier access. However, third-party access providers have asked regulators for interconnection to LEC facilities primarily to offer switched transport service. If such interconnection is granted, both the value of third-party-provided access and competition for access will increase.

Bypass of switched access falls into three categories: totally private networks, the use of non-LEC facilities bypass between end users and ICs, and the use of LEC special access facilities between end users and ICs. A number of totally private networks have been built. These were generally constructed for data communications or other specialized needs however. Such networks are of tertiary significance as factor inputs for ICs and, therefore, for our purposes, they are of little concern. Facilities bypass can occur through an IC or customer owned line, but it is increasingly obtained through third-party providers. Third-party or alternate access providers construct localized fiber optic networks, usually in downtown or other business districts, which are connected to the ICs' networks. Special access lines provided by the LECs are used for data and point-to-point private line service, as well as switched access charge avoidance. Although special access is thought to currently account for 70-80 percent of total bypass (U.S. Federal-State Joint Board (1991)), facilities bypass is sufficient to hold LEC prices in check.

Special access is purchased for a variety of uses, not all of which are consistent with switched access charge avoidance. For instance, broadcasters lease audio and video transmission lines to link up to each other and to their affiliated network. Also, computer communications are enhanced by digital data lines. These services require features that switched access cannot provide (high speeds and digital transmission), and, in fact, they often do not benefit from the ability to be switched. While data communications is growing, it does not represent a substantial portion of the total LEC-handled traffic.

The types of special access more suited to switched access charge avoidance are voice grade lines, WATS lines, and DS1 (high capacity) connections. Voice grade lines and WATS lines are specifically designed to carry voice traffic. DS1 connections have greater capacity, enabling up to 24 simultaneous voice-grade connections. A higher capacity connection, DS3, is essentially equivalent to 28 DS1 connections. However, quantity data for DS3 connections were unavailable for this study. WATS lines are a hybrid of special and switched access, since customers are charged a monthly fee and a usage fee for local transport and switching but are not charged the Carrier Common Line Charge. High speed data communications also use DS1 connections. The fraction of DS1 connections used for data transmission is unknown however. While the mix of special access services changed since 1988, in aggregate, voice-grade lines, WATS lines and DS1 connections comprise the great majority of special access use for the time period of the data used in this study.

3.   A Model of Inter-Exchange Carrier Bypass Incentives

The term "bypass" has been used to describe many activities; in this paper it is defined somewhat more narrowly. The bypass decisions addressed here pertain to the method of connection the IC chooses for an end user. For each customer connection, ICs are assumed to choose either to purchase switched access or bypass the LEC switched network. An IC bypasser can build dedicated facilities between the IC's network and the customer's premises, or it can gain connection through the lease of a dedicated line, usually from the LEC under a special access arrangement. Both of these bypass alternatives represent continued use of the IC's network.

ICs are assumed to choose factor input levels to minimize the total costs, C, of providing a certain level of service to their end users. Let i index ICs. If switched access, A_i, and bypass, B_i, are closely substitutable factor inputs, then the IC_i will purchase these inputs in the proportion that equates their marginal costs,

$$\frac{\partial C_i}{\partial B_i} = \frac{\partial C_i}{\partial A_i}. \tag{1}$$

Initially, the marginal cost to the IC of switched access is assumed to be a fixed constant, ordinarily its nominal price. The marginal cost of bypass is increasing with the amount of bypass.[10] Equation (1) has an interior solution if the marginal cost of bypass is below the marginal cost of LEC access for the first customer and above that for the last.

Let r be the price of switched access and c be the constant marginal cost to the LEC of providing this access. Then total switched access expenditures for IC_i are $r A_i$ and marginal IC costs of LEC switched access are

$$\frac{\partial C_i}{\partial A_i} = r + A_i \frac{dr}{dA_i}. \tag{2}$$

The derivative dr/dA_i is determined by assuming that the total revenue, R, from switched access is constant, and the price is determined by dividing switched access revenue by the total switched access demanded, $r = R / \Sigma_j A_j$. The effect of a change in A_i on r is derived by r differentiated with respect to A_i while holding R and A_k constant for $k \neq i$, so that

$$\frac{dr}{dA_i} = -\frac{R}{(\Sigma_j A_j)^2} = -\frac{r}{\Sigma_j A_j}. \tag{3}$$

Finally, combining equations (1), (2) and (3) yields:

$$\frac{\partial C_i}{\partial B_i} = r(1 - w_i), \tag{4}$$

where w_i is IC_i's share of switched access, $w_i = A_i / \Sigma_j A_j$.

---

[10] The marginal cost to the IC of bypass along any particular route is likely to decrease with respect to the quantity of calls or even bypass circuits <u>along that route</u>. The marginal cost of bypass will be increasing <u>as routes are added</u>; additional routes will be longer with less traffic.

Equation (4) indicates that ICs choose the level of switched access and bypass such that the marginal cost of bypass is equated with a value which can be less than the price of switched access. Moreover, this shadow price varies inversely with the IC's share of LEC switched access. In essence, a fixed revenue level for LECs from switched access causes an IC to have a diminished incentive to bypass, and this effect is greater for a larger IC. Consider the monopsonist IC and the fringe IC as polar opposites. A monopsonist IC ($w_i = 1$) has a shadow price of switched access equal to zero and the revenue is transferred as a lump sum tax. The fringe IC ($w_i \approx 0$) has a shadow price close to the full switched access price, r.

The source of the difference in shadow prices between small and large ICs is important to understand. This form of regulation, seeking a constant dollar amount of switched access revenue, confers a strategic compliment attribute to switched access. As one IC uses more switched access, the switched access price to all users falls, and thus, all ICs' costs fall. As an IC's share of switched access rises, the portion of the complementarily that is internalized also rises. For a switched access monopsonist, this complementarity is completely internalized; for a fringe competitor it, is trivial to its decision process.

This model is, of course, a simplification of the actual market for access, and real world factors may abrogate the Brandon Effect. Some of the more obvious potential criticisms will be considered and reconciled with the model presented. These criticisms stem from: the different means of bypassing switched access charges, the potential endogeneity of the switched access share and the move toward price-cap regulation.

First, bypass in the model applies to all forms of switched access avoidance, but, in the tests below, bypass is identified with special access. The important issue is whether, absent the Brandon Effect, the size of the IC will greatly affect the choice of the form of bypass. LEC provided special access is often provided in the same way with the same technology as third-party or IC-provided facilities bypass. Special access should be an excellent proxy for bypass in total. In addition, as noted earlier, special access constitutes the great majority of bypass.

Second, the analysis takes IC switched access shares as exogenous, yet the Brandon Effect could be a determinant of the shares. The feedback would tend to increase IC switched access share differentials, since smaller ICs are more likely to opt for bypass instead of switched access. The endogeneity is likely to be small relative to the effects of other factors in the telecommunications industry during this time period however (e.g., IC price

8

differentials). Since AT&T's share of switched access has fallen dramatically, this feedback appears to be small relative to other factors. In addition, because the feedback would cause an accentuating rather than countervailing effect, the model can still be unambiguously tested.

Third, the move to "price-cap regulation" at the Federal level does not affect the applicability of the analysis. AT&T's incentives toward bypass should not have changed substantially when rate-of-return regulation was replaced by "price-cap regulation." LECs have only faced "price-cap regulation" since January of 1991.[11] Moreover, in both cases, the form of "price-cap regulation" adopted contains strong rate-of-return features through sharing mechanisms beyond certain rate-of-return levels. The fixed dollar revenue framework still exists.

4.   Empirical Tests

The analysis above implies that the relevant switched access price measure to ICs is not the posted nominal price. The shadow price depends on the nominal price and the IC's relative share of all switched access. The determinants of IC access demand and supply are estimated in order to conduct two tests of this hypothesis. First, a test for positive correlation between switched access demand and switched access share of expenditures, *ceteris paribus*, is conducted. This is performed by a t test in a multiple regression. Second, specification tests comparing a demand model employing the shadow price of switched access to a demand model employing the nominal price are conducted using a series of nonnested J tests.

The principle data source for these tests is proprietary to Southwestern Bell Telephone Co., obtained under a nondisclosure agreement. These data are monthly purchases from January 1989 through December 1991 of switched and special access usage from Southwestern Bell by various ICs for each state in which Southwestern Bell operates.[12] Data are generally available for AT&T, MCI, Sprint and an aggregation of all other carriers. Special access quantity data exist only for AT&T and the aggregation of non-AT&T carriers (called the Other Common Carriers or OCCs). The variables available are revenues and quantities of both switched and special access usage.

---

[11] Price-caps for LECs were established in CC Docket No. 87-313 (Released Oct. 4, 1990).

[12] These are Arkansas, Kansas, Missouri, Oklahoma, and Texas.

Since special access is the primary mode of switched access avoidance, it is used as a surrogate for total bypass. Also available, but not at the individual IC level, are price indices for switched and special access for each month and state. Information on the demand for long-distance service and cost of inputs into the production of access are also used.

Estimating individual factor demand equations for switched and special access is problematic for two reasons. First, the data are not rich enough to estimate reliably the necessary parameters. The prices of both factors of production are likely to enter both factor demand equations. Since these prices are likely to be endogenous, separate instrumental variables would be required for each price variable. Such instrumental variables are not available. Second, the switched access expenditure share by IC, a key explanatory variable, is almost surely correlated to the level of switched access demand. Again, the advisable strategy is to find instrumental variables for the share. However, it is difficult to imagine a variable that affects this share that does not belong in the demand equation itself.

Alternatively, the ratio of the factors of demand is estimated as a function of the ratio of factor prices and other variables. The coefficient of the price ratio yields an elasticity of substitution between switched access and bypass. Using this approach, instrumental variables are needed for only one variable, the price ratio, at the cost of the assumption of a constant elasticity of substitution. An IC's relative factor proportions of switched access and bypass is not likely to be affected by the IC's share of total switched access expenditures (other than through the shadow price of switched access). Thus, for AT&T and the OCCs,

$$\frac{QtySwAcc_{kt}^{ATT}}{QtyBypass_{kt}^{ATT}} = f^{ATT}\left[\frac{PrcSwAcc_{kt}^{ATT}}{PrcBypass_{kt}^{ATT}}, SwAccShr_{kt}^{ATT}, X_{kt}\right] + \epsilon_{kt}^{ATT} \qquad (5)$$

$$\frac{QtySwAcc_{kt}^{OCC}}{QtyBypass_{kt}^{OCC}} = f^{OCC}\left[\frac{PrcSwAcc_{kt}^{OCC}}{PrcBypass_{kt}^{OCC}}, SwAccShr_{kt}^{OCC}, X_{kt}\right] + \epsilon_{kt}^{OCC} \qquad (6)$$

are estimated, where X is a vector of exogenous factor demand shifting variables and k and t subscript state and month.

Economists often assume that factor input prices are determined exogenously from factor demand determination. However, for two different reasons, the price ratios in equations (5)-(6) could be endogenous to the quantity ratios. First, either the LEC could exercise market power in switched access usage or AT&T could exercise a degree of monopsony power. If either of these is the case, price will be a function of the quantity demanded. Second, both prices in these ratios are set by regulators seeking revenues to "recover" fixed costs; if demand decreases, prices will rise in order to satisfy the fixed total revenue level or fixed revenue requirement. Indeed, this is exactly the type of assumption necessary for the existence of the Brandon Effect. Thus, supply price determination equations,

$$\frac{PrcSwAcc_{kt}^{ATT}}{PrcBypass_{kt}^{ATT}} = g^{ATT}\left[\frac{QtySwAcc_{kt}^{ATT} + QtySwAcc_{kt}^{OCC}}{QtyBypass_{kt}^{ATT} + QtyBypass_{kt}^{OCC}}, Z_{kt}\right] + v_{kt}^{ATT} \qquad (7)$$

$$\frac{PrcSwAcc_{kt}^{OCC}}{PrcBypass_{kt}^{OCC}} = g^{OCC}\left[\frac{QtySwAcc_{kt}^{ATT} + QtySwAcc_{kt}^{OCC}}{QtyBypass_{kt}^{ATT} + QtyBypass_{kt}^{OCC}}, Z_{kt}\right] + v_{kt}^{OCC} \qquad (8)$$

are also estimated, where Z represents a vector of exogenous LEC supply shifting variables correlated with the price ratio. Equations (5)-(8) form a system of simultaneous equations to be estimated by instrumental variables techniques.

Data Description

The data available provide measures of quantity and price ratios from which equations (5)-(8) can be estimated. The appendix provides a description of the construction of the variables used in this study. Actual expenditures are divided by actual quantities to obtain average prices for switched and special access demand. The ratio of the actual quantities can be regressed against the ratio of these average prices paid. This construction suffers because aggregating various forms of special access is problematic. The most common types of special access used to avoid switched access charges are single line WATS/voice grade connections and multiple circuit DS1 connections. DS1 trunks can handle up to 24 different voice grade lines (they are also used for high speed data transmission), but since additional charges are incurred as additional lines are activated, often some lines are left unused. Concrete data on the average number of lines used per DS1 trunk does not exist; however, conversations with Southwestern Bell experts lead us to believe that, on average, approximately 16 circuits are used per DS1 connection. Obviously, this number can vary over time, across ICs, or across states; unfortunately, however, we have no information on the size or direction of the variation. Thus, special access lines are aggregated as the sum of the WATS lines, voice-grade lines and 16 times DS1 lines. The benefit of this construction is that digital data lines are not included and the price measures are specific to the IC.

The construction of the switched access share variable requires some discussion. First, while the switched access share for AT&T is directly calculated as AT&T's switched access expenditure divided by total switched access expenditure, the corresponding value for the OCCs is slightly more complicated. The switched access share for the OCCs is calculated as the weighted average of the individual share's for MCI, Sprint and other ICs, where the weights are the fraction of OCC expenditure represented by MCI, Sprint or the other ICs. Furthermore, since the other ICs share itself constitutes an aggregation of many small firms, its share is divided by ten in order to approximate their average share. Second, the switched access share of revenue is possibly correlated with the ratio of switched to special access quantity by construction (rather than due to the Brandon Effect). To avoid this occurrence, for each IC and state in the sample, the IC's average share over the other four states is substituted.

The variables in X, those that shift factor demand for switched access relative to special access, include variables affecting end-user demand and variables measuring the level of other IC factor inputs. Real disposable income per capita is used to capture income effects and the number of residential and nonresidential lines are included to reflect the size of these markets. Bypass is much more likely to occur in the provision of IC service to business rather than residential customers; business customers in different industries have greater opportunities for bypass based on their use of telecommunications. To measure these industry differences, the number of employees in each of eight broad industry categories are included as possible demand-shifting variables. While the costs of other IC factor inputs could affect the switched access to special access ratio, only data reflecting the average cost of debt from the yields to maturity on the AT&Ts' corporate bonds are available.

The variables in Z, those that shift the relative prices of switched and special access, include prices of inputs into the production of both types of access, the Subscriber Line Charge (SLC), and other variables intended to capture the workings of the regulatory process. For prices of inputs into the production of access, the wage of telecommunications workers, the cost of debt for Southwestern Bell and the prices of nonbroadcast communications transmission equipment and central office switching equipment are used. Since the SLC was intended to partially replace the switched access charge as a method of local loop cost recovery, increases in the SLC are expected to be concurrent with decreases in the price of switched access. Other regulatory variables include "excess" returns to LEC switched and special access, and the equity income of large long distance companies and LECs. "Excess" returns (actual returns above the target or allowed rate of return) are expected to lead to lower access prices in the subsequent rate order. Finally, an increase in the switched access price can be thought of as a transfer from ICs to LECs. If regulators are interested in maintaining the financial viability of both types of companies, then past financial distress of LECs (ICs) will lead to future higher (lower) switched access prices (regulators are assumed to have much less discretion with special access prices). Financial distress is measured for ICs and LECs as the income (both dividends and capital gains) generated by holding stock in a portfolio including AT&T and MCI and the seven regional Bell Holding Companies respectively. In order to allow for a form of regulatory lag, all of these variables, except the SLC, are computed as moving averages of values over the past six months.

Estimation Issues

The applicability of instrumental variables methods to the existing data has already been noted. Specifically, the variables exogenous to the system, X and Z, are used as instruments. First stage regression results are not reported.

Other estimation issues include possible autocorrelation and heteroskedasticity. Existence of either of these problems will lead to inefficient estimation and biased standard errors, rendering inference testing problematic. First, estimated correlations between the error term and lags of the error term for the same state indicate that autocorrelation is present. Autocorrelation is corrected for by quasi-first differencing the data. Second, since an observation represents the average across individuals in a state, and the states in the sample have significant variation in population, the standard error of a variable for a large state will be smaller than for a small state. This leads to a smaller variance of the standard error of the regression for large states relative to small states. The remedy

13

employed here for this form of heteroskedasticity is to weight observations by the population of the state it represents.

Almost all variables included in the regressions are the natural logarithm of the underlying variable; the exceptions, the net income and "excess" returns variables in the price equations, are due to the existence of negative values of these variables. Thus, coefficient estimates usually can be interpreted as elasticities and, specifically, the coefficient on price in the quantity equations is interpreted as the elasticity of substitution. The magnitude of the coefficients on the net income and "excess" returns are more difficult to interpret.

5.   Empirical Results

This section presents results from estimation of equations (5)-(8) and nonnested tests. Generally, tests strongly, but not uniformly, confirm the presence of the Brandon Effect.

Regression Results

Table 1 reports two stage least squares (2SLS) coefficient estimates of equations (5)-(8). Durbin-Wu-Hausman tests reject at a high confidence level the hypothesis that endogeneity between the price ratio and the quantity ratio will not cause OLS estimates to be inconsistent (Hausman (1978)) The specification presented is the result of a number of specification tests.

In the quantity-ratio equations, the price ratio enters negatively and the switched access share enters positively for both AT&T and the OCCs. However, these coefficients are significant only for AT&T. The t tests on the switched access share confirm the existence of the Brandon Effect, at least for AT&T. Also, the shadow price of switched access is inversely related to the switched access share, suggesting that the elasticity of substitution defined for shadow prices is larger (in absolute terms) than the coefficient of the price ratio suggests. A larger shadow price elasticity of substitution is confirmed below.

Since the dependent variable is the quantity ratio, coefficients on other explanatory variables measure the effect of these variables on factor demand for switched access relative to the factor demand for special access. An insignificant coefficient could imply that the variable does not have an appreciable effect on factor demand.

14

Alternatively, insignificance could be interpreted as implying that the magnitudes of these variables for switched and special access are comparable.

Higher per capita income increases the demand for switched access relative to special access for both AT&T and the OCCs. The cost of debt (measured as the yield to maturity on corporate bonds) has no effect for either AT&T or the OCCs. The effect of residential and nonresidential lines have opposite effects for AT&T and the OCCs. A greater number of residential lines decreases the switched- to special-access ratio for AT&T and increases it for the OCCs. However, a greater number of nonresidential lines increases the switched to special access ratio for AT&T and decreases it for the OCCs. These nonresidential lines are almost exclusively nonspecial access business lines. Since businesses tend to use more long distance than residences and long distance service over these lines entails switched access, a positive coefficient is expected.

Measures of employment in different sectors of the state's economy are intended to capture differences in demand by long distance customers. Generally, coefficients tend to have the same signs for both AT&T and the OCCs. A positive (negative) coefficient indicates that the sector uses more (less) switched access relative to special access than the average sector. Construction and transportation and public utilities use relatively more switched access, while trade, and, perhaps, finance, insurance and real estate and services, use relatively more special access. Since larger telecommunications users (and the ICs that serve them) have the best opportunity and motive for bypass, more of these users are expected to increase the relative share of special access. Our results are consistent with this expectation, since many of the most telecommunications intensive sectors reported by Crandall (1991) can be classified as trade and finance, insurance and real estate.[13]

The coefficients also tend to have the same sign for both AT&T and the OCCs in the price ratio equation. The quantity ratio enters negatively and significantly as expected if regulators attempted to maintain a constant amount of revenue for LECs from switched access. The coefficient of the SLC is positive, contrary to expectation, but not significant. The cost of debt and the price of transmission equipment raise the price of switched access relative to special access, while the price of central office switching equipment lowers it. Industry wages have no

---

[13] The telecommunications intensive sectors reported in Crandall (1991) are financial services; retail and wholesale trade; hotels and motels; health, education, and social services; transportation; eating and drinking places; real estate and rentals.

effect on relative prices. The excess returns coefficients generally have the expected signs. High past special (switched) access excess returns tend to decrease the relative price of special (switched) access. However, the equity income coefficients have mixed signs and never approach significance.

Nonnested Tests

Next, nonnested J tests (Davidson and MacKinnon (1981)) of the nominal price versus the shadow price constructed as one minus the IC's switched access share times the nominal price ratio are presented. The competing hypotheses are that the nominal and shadow price ratio constructions describe the process that generated the data. Since the log of the switched to special access price ratio is not linearly nested within the log of the shadow price ratio, nonnested testing techniques are appropriate.

Generally, nonnested tests attempt to distinguish between two models of the data where neither model is a linear extension of the other (e.g. nominal versus shadow price). This is accomplished by artificially nesting both hypothesized models within a more general model. The dependent variable is regressed against one model plus α times the other model. However, when the two models share some exogenous variables, this leads to an underidentified equation. The solution is to replace the unknown parameters of the model not being tested with consistent estimates, usually the predicted values from this model's specification. A t test on whether α is different from zero indicates whether the information in the predicted values helps "explain" the data. An α different from zero implies that, without this information, the model being tested is missspecified. By reversing which model's predicted values are included, both specifications can be tested. With these procedures, it is possible to reject neither model or to reject both as missspecified.

In the present application, the possible endogeneity of the switched access share can also be better addressed by the use of J tests. Because the switched access share could be correlated with the error terms by construction, equations (5) and (6) use the ratio of switched to special access demand as the dependent variable and switched access shares for one state were computed using information from the other states. This purges the variables of much of the presumed spurious correlation. In the J test specifications, the switched access shares are incorporated

16

in the shadow prices and these, in turn, are projected onto the instrumental variables. These instrumental variables purge both the nominal price and the switched access share of their possible correlation with the error term.

Table 2 reports the J test results. The nominal price model is rejected for AT&T but not for the OCCs, and the shadow price model is not rejected for either AT&T or the OCCs. These tests imply that either the nominal price or the shadow price describe the data for the OCCs, but only the shadow price describes the AT&T data. The failure to reject either model for the OCCs is probably linked to the relatively small variation in the switched access share for the average OCC firm. For the OCCs, the constructed shadow price ratio and nominal price ratio are highly correlated.

Given these results, examining the price ratio coefficients in the competing models is enlightening. These are reported in table 3. Coefficients for X are not reported but remain virtually unchanged from table 1. For the OCCs, there is little difference in the estimated price elasticities. For AT&T, the estimated elasticities are somewhat greater (in absolute terms) for the shadow price model than for the nominal price. This is to be expected if the Brandon Effect guides AT&T decision-making.

Other Specifications

Two other specifications of the data were also tested with qualitatively the same results. First, as discussed above, WATS service only avoids a portion of the switched access charges. Equations (5)-(8) were estimated with WATS lines excluded from the special access quantity with nearly identical results. Second, Southwestern Bell constructs indices of switched and special access prices aggregated across all purchasers that provide an independent measure of the switched to special price ratio. Also, these indices provide a different measure of quantity by dividing access revenue by the relevant price index. Specifications using these price and quantity indices yielded results which were less precise, but, nonetheless, similar to those reported above.

6.   Conclusion

This paper describes, models and tests for the so-called Brandon Effect. This effect arises when the price for an input with close substitutes is set above marginal costs so as to generate a fixed dollar amount of revenue

17

to the seller. The model presented is simple and similar to (although more explicit than) descriptions presented elsewhere. The formula for an IC's shadow price for switched access is deduced from the model as the nominal price times one minus the IC's share of the total switched access demand. Tests for the Brandon Effect center on whether switched access share has the expected effect on the demand for switched access. While the test results presented do not uniformly confirm this hypothesis, they clearly support it.

The results raise issues for business and public policy. First, models of bypass behavior that ignore the Brandon Effect are likely to overstate actual levels of bypass, particularly bypass by AT&T. Second, over time as AT&T's share of total switched access falls, AT&T's shadow price of switched access will rise and its incentive to bypass will increase. The incentive to bypass by MCI and Sprint will fall over time as their switched access shares rise. Third, regulatory policy changes that render a constant dollar revenue target unrealistic or unattainable would eliminate the Brandon Effect mechanism. A true form of price-caps or incentive regulation (without rate-of-return elements) would eliminate the switched access fixed dollar framework. Likewise, competition from third-party access providers could erode the market power necessary to achieve the fixed dollar amount if they are granted favorable LEC interconnection opportunities by regulators. In either case, the incentive to bypass would increase for all ICs because nominal prices, and not the lower shadow switched access prices constructed above, would reflect true opportunity costs.

Aside from direct tests for the existence of the Brandon Effect, this paper raises some issues for access demand estimation. Often, access demand estimates for regulatory proceedings are derived from single equation OLS models.[14] The empirical work presented here suggests that both the price of switched access and the price of special access are endogenous to the quantity of switched access demanded. Single equation models that ignore these effects could be missspecified, leading to inconsistent estimates.

---

[14] See Gatto, et al. (1988) and the studies cited therein.

References

Bell Communication Research, *The Impact of End User Charges on Bypass and Universal Service* September 1984.

Bradley, Stephen P. and Hausman, Jerry A. ed., *Future Competition in Telecommunications* (Harvard Business School Pres, Boston, MA 1989).

Brandon, Paul S., "NTS Separations Allocators: Usage-Based or Usage Independent," AT&T Tariffs and Costs; June 1, 1982 Unpublished Manuscript.

Britman, Michael K., Pehrsson, Kirston, M., and Rohlfs, J. H., *Bypass and Growth of Demand for Switched Access* Shooshan and Jackson, Inc., Washington, DC 1989.

Brock, Gerald W., *The Telecommunications Industry: The Dynamics of Market Structure* (Harvard University Press, Cambridge, MA 1981).

Brock, Gerald W., "Bypass and the Local Exchange: A Quantitative Assessment," Federal Communications Commission, Office of Plans and Policy, Working Paper Series No. 12, Washington, DC September 1984.

Crandall, Robert W., *After the Breakup* (Brookings Institution, Washington, DC 1991).

Davidson, R. and MacKinnon, J., "Several Tests for Model Specification in the Presence of Multiple Alternatives," *Econometrica* 49 (1981) 781-793.

Faulhaber, Gerald R., *Telecommunications in Turmoil* (Ballinger Publishing Co., Cambridge, MA 1987).

Gatto, Joseph P., Langin-Hooper, Jerry, Robinson, Paul B. and Tyan, Holly, "Interstate Switched Access Demand Analysis", *Information Economics and Policy* 3 (1988) 333-358.

Grandstaff, Peter J. and Watters, John S., "Switched Access Competition in U.S. Telephony: Evidence and Interpretation," *Review of Business* (Spring 1989) 19-26.

Griffen, James, "The Welfare Implications of Externalities and Price Elasticities for Telecommunications Pricing," *Review of Economics and Statistics* 64 (1982).

Hausman, Jerry A. "Specification Tests in Econometrics," *Econometrica* (Nov. 1978) 1251-1272.

Jackson, C. L. and Rohlfs, J. H., *Access Charging and Bypass Adoption* Shooshan and Jackson, Inc., Washington, DC 1985.

Johnson, Leland, *Competition and Cross-Subsidization in the Telephone Industry* The Rand Corporation, Santa

    Monica, CA 1982.

Kasserman, David L., Mayo, John W. and Flynn, Joseph E., "Cross-Substitution in Telecommunications: Beyond

    the Universal Service Fairy Tale," *Journal of Regulatory Economics* 2 (1990).

Kahn, Alfred E. and Shew, William B., "Current Issues in Telecommunications Regulation: Pricing," *Yale Journal*

    on Regulation 4 (1987).

Katz, Michael and Willig, Robert D., "The Effects of Capped NTS Charges on Long Distance Competition,"

    mimeo (1985).

Larson, Alexander C. and Mudd, Douglas R., "Collocation and Telecommunications Policy: A Fostering of

    Competition on the Merits," *California Western Law Review* 28 (1992).

Parsons, Steven G. and Ward, Michael R., "Bypass Incentives When Regulators Impose a Fixed Dollar Revenue

    Requirement for Access," Unpublished Manuscript (July 1991).

Rohlfs, Jeffrey, "Economically Efficient Bell System Pricing," Bell Laboratories Discussion Paper (1979).

Simnett, Richard E., "Contestable Markets and Telecommunications," in *Deregulation and Diversification of*

    Utilities, Michael A. Crew (ed.) (Kluwer Academic Publishers Boston, MA, 1988).

Taylor, Lester D., *Telecommunications Demand: A Survey and Critique* (Ballinger Publishing Company,

    Cambridge, MA 1980).

Temin, Peter, *The Fall of the Bell System* (Cambridge University Press, New York NY 1987).

Temin, Peter and Peter, Geoffrey, "Cross-Substitution in the Telephone Network," *Willamete Law Review* 21

    (1985a).

Temin, Peter and Peter, Geoffrey, "Is History Stranger than Theory? The Origins of Telephone Separations,"

    Economic History 75 (1985b).

U.S. Federal Communications Commission, *Statistics of Communications Common Carriers*, Washington, DC: U.S.

    Government Publishing Office, various years.

U.S. Federal-State Joint Board, *Monitoring Report* (CC Docket No. 87-339) Washington, DC, January 1991.

United States Telephone Association, *Bypass Study* 1984.

Weisman, Dennis L., "Default Capacity Tariffs: Smoothing the Transitional Regulatory Asymmetries in the Telecommunications Market," *Yale Journal on Regulation* 5 (1988) 149-178.

Weisman, Dennis L. and Kridel Donald J., "Forecasting Competitive Entry: The Case of Bypass Adoption in Telecommunications," *International Journal of Forecasting* 6 (1990) 65-74.

Wenders, John T., *The Economics of Telecommunications* (Ballinger Publishing Company, Cambridge, MA 1987.

Wenders, John T. and Egan, Bruce L., "The Implications of Economic Efficiency for US Telecommunications Policy," *Telecommunications Policy* 10 (March 1986) 33-40.

Appendix Definitions of Variables

Ratio of Switched to Special Access Quantity - is the number of minutes of use (MOU) of switched access divided by the number of lines of special access. The number of special access lines was computed as the sum of WATS, voice grade and sixteen times DS1 (source: Southwestern Bell).

Ratio of Switched to Special Access Price - is the ratio of the average expenditure per MOU of switched access divided by the average expenditure per line of special access. Special access expenditures used here are total special access expenditures minus an estimate of digital data expenditures. The number of special access lines was computed as the sum of WATS, voice grade and sixteen times DS1 (source: Southwestern Bell).

Switched Access Share - is the ratio of the IC's switched access expenditures to the sum of all IC switched access expenditures. To avoid possible spurious correlation with the dependent variable, the ratio for any state is defined as this ratio computed for expenditures in all other states (source: Southwestern Bell).

Residential and Non-Residential Lines - are the number of residential and non-residential lines Southwestern Bell serves in the state (source: Southwestern Bell).

Income per capita - is disposable personal income per capita in the state for the quarter (source: Survey of Current Business)

Cost of Debt - is the average real yield to maturity on the firms' corporate bonds. Conversion from nominal to real rates was accomplished by deflating a bond's yield to maturity by the yield to maturity on a comparably lived government bond (source: Moody's).

Employment in a sector of the economy - is the number of people employed in the sector in the state. The eight sectors are: Mining; Construction; Manufacturing; Transportation and Public Utilities; Finance, Insurance and Real Estate; Services; and Government (source: Employment and Earnings).

Subscriber Line Charge - is the real national average subscriber line charge (source: Monitoring Report).

Telephone Worker Wage - is the real wage of nonprofessional telecommunications workers (source: Employment and Earnings).

Price of Central Office Switching Equipment and Transmission Equipment - are real price indices for central office switching equipment and non-broadcast communications transmission equipment (source: Producer Price Indexes).

Long Distance and Bell Operating Company Equity Income - are the real dollar returns, including capital gains and dividend payments, to holding, in proportion to their equity value, stock in AT&T and MCI and stock in the seven Bell operating companies (source: Center for Research on Security Prices).

Special and Switched Access Excess Return - are the real values of actual returns in excess of the allowed return for Southwestern Bell special and switched access service (source: Southwestern Bell).

Table 1
Demand Determined by
Nominal Price and Switched Access Share
2SLS Estimates

Variable	AT&T Quantity Ratio	OCCs Quantity Ratio	Variable	AT&T Price Ratio	OCCs Price Ratio
Intercept	-2.13	-5.80	Intercept	0.44	-7.63
	(2.45)	(2.39)		(1.48)	(4.29)
Price Ratio	-0.22[7]	-0.20	Quantity Ratio	-0.12[2]	-1.09[1]
	(0.12)	(0.18)		(0.05)	(0.30)
Switched Access	1.16[1]	0.22	Subscriber Line	0.23	1.58
Share	(0.30)	(0.94)	Charge	(0.35)	(1.19)
Income per capita	1.21[2]	1.98[4]	Telecommunications	0.19	-3.49
	(0.50)	(0.95)	Worker Wage	(1.32)	(4.56)
Corporate Bond	0.09		SWBT Corp. Bond	8.10[3]	22.05[8]
Yield to Maturity	(1.22)		Yield to Maturity	(3.71)	(12.63)
Residential Lines	-1.08[8]	1.67	Price of Transmission	1.38	13.16[1]
	(0.61)	(1.20)	Equipment	(0.89)	(3.70)
Non-Residential	1.07[1]	-3.97[1]	Price of Switching	-1.56[7]	1.63
Lines	(0.32)	(0.94)	Equipment	(0.86)	(2.26)
Mining	0.11[3]	0.49[1]	Special Access	-1.58[1]	-6.25[1]
Employment	(0.05)	(0.10)	Excess Returns	(0.33)	(1.67)
Construction	0.36[1]	-0.08	Switched Access	0.19	1.15[5]
Employment	(0.12)	(0.22)	Excess Returns	(0.14)	(0.59)
Manufacturing	0.17	0.27	Long Dist. Company	-1.03	1.53
Employment	(0.15)	(0.41)	Equity Income	(3.01)	(11.27)
Transportation & Publ.	0.88[4]	2.08[2]	Bell Oper. Company	1.51	2.27
Util. Employment	(0.43)	(0.85)	Equity Income	(1.87)	(6.57)
Retail & Wholesale	-1.63[1]	-1.19			
Trade Employment	(0.40)	(0.78)			
Finance, Insurance, &	-0.71[1]	1.94[1]			
& Real Estate Empl.	(0.24)	(0.57)			
Services	0.41	-1.55[1]			
Employment	(0.28)	(0.56)			
Government	0.16	0.10			
Employment	(0.11)	(0.20)			
Rho	0.11	0.53		0.59	0.79
Number of Obs.	175	175	Number of Obs.	175	175
Adjusted R^2	.92	.92	Adjusted R^2	.35	.09

Standard errors are in parentheses and superscripts denote significance levels for a two-tailed test if less than 10%. Observations are weighted by state population.

Table 2
Nonnested J Test Results
Nominal versus Shadow Price Models

Estimate of Alpha	Nominal Price Model	Shadow Price Model
AT&T	1.40[1]	-0.88
	(0.40)	(0.69)
OCCs	1.53	-0.56
	(4.30)	(4.48)

This table presents coefficients and standard errors of α in the equation

$$y = x_1 \beta_1 + \alpha x_2 \hat{\beta}_2 + \epsilon$$

where subscripts denote the competing models describing the data generating process. Superscripts reported in the table denote significance levels for a two-tailed test of α greater than zero if less than 10 percent.

Table 3
Elasticities of Substitution
in Competing Models

Elasticity of Substitution	Nominal Price Model	Shadow Price Model
AT&T	-0.28[3]	-0.34[1]
	(0.13)	(0.09)
OCCs	-0.19	-0.21
	(0.17)	(0.18)

Standard errors are in parentheses and superscripts denote significance levels for a two-tailed test if less than 10%. Observations are weighted by state population.